Ken Knight has been writing since his desk was pushed across the hall from Grade 3 to 4 and as part of various careers since then.

A graduate of the University of Calgary, Knight enjoys writing more than any other thing and creates a poem, story or song every year for his family Christmas card which includes all the year's news in rhyme.

For Emily and Julie

Ken Knight

LEFTY LOOSEY RIGHTY TIGHTY

AUSTIN MACAULEY PUBLISHERS™
LONDON · CAMBRIDGE · NEW YORK · SHARJAH

Copyright © Ken Knight (2017)

The right of Ken Knight to be identified as author of this work has been asserted by him in accordance with section 77 and 78 of the Copyright, Designs and Patents Act 1988.

All rights reserved. No part of this publication may be reproduced, stored in a retrieval system, or transmitted in any form or by any means, electronic, mechanical, photocopying, recording, or otherwise, without the prior permission of the publishers.

Any person who commits any unauthorised act in relation to this publication may be liable to criminal prosecution and civil claims for damages.

A CIP catalogue record for this title is available from the British Library.

ISBN 9781786939661 (Paperback)
ISBN 9781786939678 (Hardback)
ISBN 9781786939685 (E-Book)
www.austinmacauley.com

First Published (2017)
Austin Macauley Publishers Ltd.
25 Canada Square
Canary Wharf
London
E14 5LQ

Acknowledgements

To Les, who went from, "You're writing what?" to unfailing support for my hobby and passion – this book.

Introduction

As my 50th birthday arrived and passed, my two daughters also began to inch closer to that day when they would leave the nest. One had already graduated from high school and, after a gap year and much travel, was getting ready for the first year of university. And as daughter number two began her last year of high school, I felt compelled to be ready with all kinds of worldly advice for the two girls' life journey ahead.

Perhaps if they had been boys I would have planned to go with a stereotypical scenario and sit down with them in armchairs in a dark-paneled den and pour us each a glass of good scotch for this earth-moving life conversation. Besides not being my style, I have no den, no armchairs and don't really care for scotch!

So I decided to write this book. Not so much as life advice for just my offspring, but as a bit of a guidebook for many people who are either starting out on their own or getting a fresh start later in life as I did.

I do not claim to be an expert on any of the topics about which I have written. I have merely been on the road for a while making observations and my own mistakes along the way. Along that road, I have encountered many people smarter than me (including my own daughters in some cases). I credit all of them now for their wisdom and guidance.

At one time we had a quote decaled on our kitchen wall that read, "When you stumble, make it part of the dance." I think this is a good description for the process I have gone through these last 50 or so years as I navigated that life road.

I hope that my words and thoughts make the road a little less bumpy for those that read them. Enjoy.

Be Handy

Chapter 1
Lefty Loosey, Righty Tighty

It's all fun and games until you are at the far end of a garden hose when someone asks you to turn down the water pressure and you turn it up and soak them. Or how about if you are carefully replacing one of those tiny screws that hold the battery cover onto a child's toy and you turn it the wrong way and it's lost forever in your shag carpeting?

There is no need to struggle with which way to turn a screw, jar lid or water tap. Always turn it left to loosen and right to tighten. Lefty loosey, righty tighty. Remember this little trick and you will never have to guess again. Who needs to know you have this one up your sleeve? Unless you choose to share. Probably right after someone soaks you.

Chapter 2
Measure Twice, Cut Once

My father always had plenty of little sayings as he worked in the garage or at our cabin on various projects. I know he wasn't the first to instruct, "Measure twice, cut once," but it's his voice I remember when this wisdom comes to mind. If you cut before you have checked the measurement twice (and sometimes it's worth checking even more) you will likely be back at the hardware store buying new material.

The ironic part, of course, is this advice applies to more hobbies than just wood working and really to life itself. If you are cooking, baking, scrapbooking or sewing, remember this advice. And whenever life gives you a fork in the road and calls for a decision, it pays to think twice and act once.

Chapter 3
Black to Brass

I am quite sure there are all kinds of warnings to not do electrical work yourself. In fact, I know that every time I buy a new light switch or timer it advises to consult a professional. My experience shows that a little common sense and a few rules, however, will help you to perform basic electrical tasks and avoid a hospital stay or a big invoice from an electrician.

Before you attempt anything involving electricity, turn off the power at the main breaker box in your home. If it is an electrical outlet with nothing plugged into it, plug a lamp or a hairdryer in to make sure you have the correct location turned off. Now comes the little saying to keep in your mind – black to brass. You will almost always find white wires and black wires connected to things. And silver screws and brass screws at which to connect them. The black wires go the brass screws and the white go to the silver.

Sometimes there are red wires too and green ground wires – if it gets too complicated for you, it is time to call a professional.

Chapter 4
Happy Hammering

It was 1986 when I purchased my first house and fell head-first into handyman hell. It seems almost a requirement of home ownership to spend every spare moment – and every spare dollar – at a hardware store. And in between those trips to the store, I found my way through a thousand little projects so that I emerged back at the office on Monday morning with a badge of injuries.

Our house was just a few blocks from one of the city's largest hospitals, although I had never been inside. Within weeks I was sitting in the emergency room because I had tried to hang a shelf, missed the nail with the hammer and split my thumb wide open.

Now I do hate it when people make comments like, "You are holding that hammer like a girl." What does that mean exactly? Maybe the "girl" is holding it that way because they have never been taught how to hold it properly.

A hammer is designed to be held by the handle at the far end from the heavy iron part that does the business. Don't choke it by holding it at the top. Holding it near the bottom of the handle allows the weight of the hammer to do the work and not your hand. It works like a lever.

If you are afraid of hitting your fingers or thumb like I did, try holding the nail with a pair of pliers or even a hair comb. Slick! If you have neither of those items, try poking the nail through a piece of cardboard to hold it in place. Now go hammer something and then kick some sand in people's faces. You're no girl!

Chapter 5
Picture Perfect

I still chuckle over the instructions for a piece of IKEA furniture I was assembling many years ago that informed, "It is better to be two people." Although the intent was slightly lost in the translation, I couldn't argue that having more than one person would have made the job go much easier.

One of the things I do often is to hang artwork in my home. And it is almost always better to be two people for this task – one person to hold the art at different heights and in various places while the other delivers a verdict. But when you are attempting the project alone, a few tips and tricks make it a bit easier.

Hold the piece up to the wall you are considering and decide on its proposed height. If you can manage it, use a pencil to make a very small mark at the top of the frame and roughly in the centre. If you are hanging a heavy piece and you need both hands to hold it, try locating a blemish in the paint or certain place on the wall covering and take note of it as your reference point.

Now turn the art around and measure from the top of the frame to where the hanging wire rests when you pull it tight – or where the hook or other hanging mechanism is. Mark this same distance on your wall down from the mark you made and that is where your hook or nail should go. An eraser will remove your original mark.

A good trick for keeping art hanging level is to push a straight pin into the back of the frame at the two bottom corners and snip off the heads. Use a carpenter's level – or your amazing eyesight – to level the piece and then gently push the pins into your wall. Your art will never be crooked again.

Chapter 6
Stud Sense

Have you ever hung something heavy on a wall and then arrived home to find it on the floor along with the nail or screw with which it was attached? Or had your towel bar or tissue roll holder pull out of the wall from repeated use? Things like this need to be hung from more than just the drywall or plaster on your walls. You need to locate the stud behind the wall – and I am not talking about your good-looking neighbour!

Basic building construction has wood or metal vertical studs which create the structure behind the wall surface. But finding them back there can be tricky.

I have owned a variety of fancy stud finders in my day and some work well and some do not. They are battery powered, look a bit like a taser and you slide it along the wall until it beeps to tell you it has found the edge of something thicker than the drywall – a stud. Unless you are planning to do a lot of stud finding, most people don't need to go to the expense of owning this tool.

Studs are usually placed every 16 inches from centre to centre. So if you find one you can usually measure to find its friends. This can be a challenge if you are hanging something like a towel bar that is 20 inches long, so I recommend taking this into consideration when you are buying something that is heavy or will carry a heavy load.

The drywall in your home is attached to the studs with nails or screws and these are the little gems that will help you find the studs in a low-tech way. Sometimes the plaster and paint covering the nail or screw head will 'pop' and leave a little circle on your wall. Ta da! This is the easiest way to find a stud.

If you can't see any nail pops, the next best way is to get a strong magnet and attach it to a string. If you dangle the magnet across the wall, you can watch for when it swings toward a nail or screw head. You need patience for this one!

Once you have found the stud and are ready to hang your item, remember you might need a longer nail or screw than you originally had, since it now has to go through the drywall surface – usually half an inch – and then into the wood or metal below at least an inch to make a solid attachment.

Chapter 7
Hanging Hints

When my former partner had her first apartment we learned a lot about hanging things in a rental unit where giant holes in the walls and ceilings were frowned upon. Those were the days of hanging plants in macramé holders hung from hooks in the ceiling. And 'swag' lamps, as they were called, with long cords and chains also designed to dangle from hooks in the ceiling. Yikes.

Being 18 years old at the time, we found an interesting way to hang things when we made the hole too big or it pulled out of the ceiling the first time. Facial tissue. You wrap a little piece of the tissue around the threads of the screw and turn it back into the hole. It works like a charm. And when it's time to move on and the landlord comes for an inspection, a little more tissue poked into the hole makes it nearly invisible.

Although there is not much these days we hang from the ceiling, my earlier advice applies when it comes to finding a stud, so whatever it is you are hanging up there doesn't end up on your head!

Chapter 8
Plumbing Prowess

You may never know how important your sink, faucet and toilet are to you until they are not functioning properly. And much like a new puppy, if one of them is leaking somewhere they shouldn't, it usually needs your immediate attention.

The cause of a faucet leaking could be something as simple as it has become loose or needs a new rubber washer. Sometimes you can re-tighten it with your hands or you might need a wrench. The word of the day in all plumbing is to never over-tighten! And the other important lesson is to turn off the main water underneath or at the main shut off before you start. Did I mention that you should be familiar with both of these locations in your home in every place you live?

Many newer taps have a replaceable cartridge inside them that will fix the problem. Usually the little "C" for cold and "H" for hot pop off or have a little screw and the cartridge is underneath. If it's just a simple washer that is the problem, sometimes you can just turn it over and get a good seal for a short time until you have time to find or purchase a new one.

This is a good time to make friends with the helpful people at your local hardware store or big home-improvement retailer. They are usually more than happy to give you advice and sell you the correct part. If you're afraid to take it apart before you go, snap a photo with your phone and show them the issue at the store.

Toilets are tricky and if the leak is coming from the base at the floor it might be time for a new seal. This requires the toilet to be dismantled and removed and I do not recommend this for the faint of heart! Again, your friendly retailer may be able to assist.

If you resort to calling a professional plumber and they do a great job at a reasonable price, keep their contact information handy and share it with everyone you know. A good tradesperson is worth their weight in gold.

And while we are on the glamorous subject of toilets, it's good to know about basic plunger protocol. First of all – own one. I have found that a plunger does not need to be expensive or fancy either. Just a good solid handle and the rubber part that does the business are fine. It's good to know the work happens on the upward action of the plunger as much as the downward. Never flush the toilet again before the offending clog has been loosened or you will end up with a nasty waterfall in your bathroom.

Chapter 9
Car Crazy

As a young boy, I spent many an evening and weekend in the garage with my father as he worked on our family's automobiles. He was the type of man who almost never took his car to a repair shop for anything including even the most major repairs. Mr. Bain, who lived across the lane (I'm not joking), did the same. So my father was either in his garage or Mr. Bain was in ours on many occasions.

Despite all that time being physically present, I unfortunately did not inherit or obtain by osmosis any talent for repairing cars. I was usually the one passing a tool or holding a work light and obviously very little sunk in!

What I did learn, however, was to take care of my car and make sure regular maintenance was performed. The result is I usually keep a car for around 17 years and at that point it is still running almost perfectly. But by then I am also bored with it.

I recommend everyone learn how to do basic things like keeping tires inflated, having the engine oil changed at regular intervals and topping up necessary fluids under the hood. When you buy a new vehicle, ask the seller or sales person to show you where all these things are. It might be red flag if they do not know how to show you. Most new vehicles have fancy and sometimes annoying little lights and sounds to tell you when something needs attention. Don't ignore them!

Be Smart

Chapter 10
Remember the Rainbow

When I was a kid in school trying to memorize things for an exam, I would always try to make up a crazy acronym to help me remember that long list of things. I am pretty sure I didn't come up with Mr. Roy G. Biv on my own, but it's handy nevertheless.

The serendipity of the whole thing is that most of these acronyms I still remember to this day, so I guess it was a good way to learn after all.

So here you go. The colours of a rainbow, in order, spell Roy G. Biv. Red, orange, yellow, green, blue, indigo and violet.

There are many other similar tricks to remember things like this and you can even make up your own. HOMES helps you remember the names of the Great Lakes as Huron, Ontario, Michigan, Erie and Superior. The more musically oriented of us can use Every Good Boy Deserves Fudge to remember the notes on lines from bottom to top of the treble clef and FACE for the notes in the spaces.

Chapter 11
Recover with Rice

A few years ago I was walking downtown between Christmas and New Year's Day and slipped on an icy curb. And not just a simple slip – my foot went into a storm water drain. Ouch. I thought for sure I had done major damage to my foot when it swelled to twice its normal size within minutes. After my in-laws rescued me and took me to the hospital, I was relieved to be told it was not broken. I was given a little instruction sheet with the word Rice as a heading.

If you fall or hurt yourself, remember that rest, ice, compression and elevation are your best friends to reduce inflammation and swelling. These four remedies spell RICE. Easy to remember and easy to do.

So stop what you are doing and rest the part of your body you hurt. Getting ice on the spot as fast as possible is the key to avoid bruising. Compression means wrapping a leg or arm or finger that you hurt in a bandage to stop swelling. And elevation means getting it up above your heart so all the blood doesn't go straight to the ouchy spot.

Chapter 12
Be a Brat

When influenza strikes or after a bout of food poisoning or self-induced tummy troubles, there are a very few foods you should start to introduce back to your diet until everything is settled again.

Yet another acronym will help you remember these foods – BRAT. Bananas, rice, applesauce and toast. I have recently heard this modified to be BRATY to include yogurt, so try this one also.

Your tummy will thank you for being a BRAT and not feeding it pizza or a hot dog when it's in trouble.

Chapter 13
Set a Smarter Goal

Lewis Carroll of *Alice in Wonderland* fame is often quoted as saying, "If you don't know where you are going, any road will take you there." The quote is a good summary of the exchange between Alice and the Cheshire Cat as they discuss Alice's desire for directions, although she has no idea of her destination. Silly Alice.

Many of us struggle with this same kind of confusion. It can be as simple as what to wear to the office today. I used to stand in the closet for way too long trying to decide which tie went with which shirt until finally I made a spreadsheet to sort it all out. Yes, I am weird. The spreadsheet is a tool to help me with my goal to get ready for work faster.

The decision of where to go in life can be – and usually is – much more difficult than my tie dilemma, but the same principles apply. Do you want a new job? Do you want to go to or go back to school? Do you want to start or end a relationship? A piece of paper and a pencil (or a keyboard and screen) are the greatest tools for working out one's goals. It stops the ideas from swimming around in your head when you have to commit them to paper.

Just like Alice, you need to know where you are going before you can figure out how to get there. I like writing my goals in SMART format. Yes, another handy acronym! Specific, measurable, action-oriented, realistic and timely goals are best.

So my wardrobe example might have sounded like, "By September 1, reduce my morning dressing routine by 10 minutes by establishing and wearing pre-determined tie-shirt pairings." It's specific – I'm talking about just my morning dressing routine. It's measurable – I will be leaving the house 10 minutes earlier. It's action-oriented, pretty realistic and will be completed by a specified date.

Chapter 14
Days in a Month

In the movie version of the Broadway musical *Mame*, Lucille Ball (her last movie role) proclaims in the opening number that her nephew is not supposed to arrive until December 1 and today is November 31 because yesterday was November 30. Oops.

There's a very old rhyme I was taught as a child to remember all this, long before everyone carried around a smart phone with a calendar.

Thirty days hath September, April, June and November; all the rest have 31 except February which hath but 28 and 29 in each leap year.

Now you and Lucy – rest her soul – can get it right every time.

Chapter 15
Nine Times Nine

In the world of multiplication, I am pretty sure memorizing times tables is a lost skill no longer taught in our schools. When I was a kid, our scribblers – or notebooks for those who don't remember what a scribbler is – had the times table up to 12 times 12 printed on the back cover. We were tested on these quite frequently!

It's easy to pick up a calculator or use your smart phone to solve multiplication equations, but one tip I have never forgotten is that the answer to everything up to 20 multiplied by nine always adds up nine.

Try it... two times nine equals 18 (one plus eight equals nine). 17 times nine equals 153 (one plus five plus three equals nine).

Chapter 16
Memorize for Your Mind

At some point in my adolescent schooling and in some forgotten science class I was taught the definition of a wave. And I apparently took it so seriously that I memorized it and can recite it word for word to this day. *A wave is a phenomenon by which energy propagates through nature as a result of vibratory motions.*

Why memorize seemingly useless information? This little definition is what I say out loud after I have fallen or banged my head. It reminds me that my brain is still working! And a working brain is a good thing most of the time.

So I recommend memorizing something every now and then. It could be a poem or the words to a song, or even the list of things you were going to get from the basement for when you get down there and forget why you are there. Your mind will thank you for this workout and reward you with better memory when you need it most.

Chapter 17
Prune Properly

As a young first-time home owner in an established area, I was suddenly faced with a large number of trees and shrubs that needed caring for. As with many things in life, timing is everything. If you lop off a piece of a living thing like a tree or bush at the wrong time of year you risk killing it or exposing it to disease.

Here's the trick I learned and it's easy to remember: only prune in months that have the letter 'r' in them. So that means the months of May, June, July and August are off limits. In general, it is best to cut back plants in the late fall or winter.

The reason for the timing is it minimizes sap loss – the sap is not running in the plant during dormant months – and this means less stress to the tree. It also means less chance of fungus or insects infesting the plant because they too are dormant at that time of year.

For a deciduous tree – one with leaves that fall off – it's also easier to prune when the leaves are all gone in order to be able to see what you are doing. Keep in mind that a little is better than a lot – taking away too much of a tree or shrub will also risk killing it.

Be Healthy

Chapter 18
Eat Clean

It was a few years ago now when I decided to take my fitness level up a notch and start eating better. Kyle, a colleague at work known for being very fit-conscious, was giving me some advice and he commented that he and his wife, "ate pretty clean." I had never heard that terminology before, but it is something that is widely talked about now and I try my best to do it.

Eating clean is pretty simple. That's because you choose items that primarily have one ingredient. Fresh vegetables – you never have to look for a nutrition label on those to see what has been added! Fresh meat, real cheese (not processed) and whole grains.

If everything you eat comes out of a box or package with an ingredient list that is a mile long and contains unpronounceable items, you are not eating clean. I used to blame my poor eating habits on a lack of time, but nothing says "fast food" like an apple, a green salad or a grilled piece of chicken or beef.

I get "oohs and awes" at the office constantly over the homemade soups I bring for lunch because they look and smell so great and look complicated. Only the individuals that ask for the recipes realize my favourites contain only things like fresh roasted tomatoes, onions, basil and organic low-sodium chicken broth. It takes me an hour on the weekend to make and freeze these soups and I never have to wonder what I am eating for the rest of the week.

Chapter 19
Get Great Teeth

I hope my daughters will thank me some day for the many thousands of dollars spent on their teeth when they were young. They each had two rounds of braces and various contraptions in their mouths to correct crooked teeth, bad bites and crazy jaws.

They will be thankful because good teeth get you a long way in life. Nice teeth give you the confidence to open up with a great smile. Good teeth are part of good grooming. And now there are all kinds of medical studies about the connection between dental health and general health. Taking care of your teeth by flossing along with brushing removes all that gunk from your teeth that turns into decay for your teeth, but also bad news for your body.

As a child growing up, I don't think I even knew what dental floss was. We certainly didn't have any in our home or any of my friends' homes. It was later in life that my friend Donna remarked that she flossed her teeth every day because she wanted to still have her own teeth later in life. That stuck with me. Then I looked at my parents' teeth – who never flossed – and realized what not flossing did for you.

I cringed at the very thought of visiting the dentist, where the hygienist would also comment that my teeth bled profusely when she worked on them. Lovely image isn't it? My greatest joy now that I floss daily is having the dental hygienist tell me what wonderful teeth and gums I have.

Chapter 20
Walking Works

I was in the best condition of my life as a teenager with a part-time job carrying out groceries to people's cars. I walked for a living. I walked to work, walked in and out of the store all day long and then walked home. These days there are thousands of books, websites and doctor shows talking about the benefits of walking. Human beings have been doing it since time began and it doesn't require any equipment or training!

One of the reasons I personally find walking so great is I have, over the years, tried having a gym membership and my own fitness equipment at home. I would be embarrassed to calculate the amount of money wasted on both. The only bright sides were some lucky gym owners never saw my face and still collected my money, and a few people walked away with pristine unused equipment when I finally gave in and sold it.

We even had a lunch time fitness class right at my place of work, which I did faithfully attend for a few years. But my incoordination and eagerness to keep up with attendees much younger than me always ended in some kind of pulled muscle or other hurt part of my body. I just find walking to be something I can do exactly at my own pace, choosing my own route and even the desired amount of time.

You don't need to run marathons. A walk around the block after dinner or a lunch time stroll will do the trick. Most "experts" say 30 minutes each day is enough and it can even be broken into three walks for 10 minutes. Take the stairs, park far away from where you are going and just go for a walk!

It is also very gratifying to use technology to track your steps, since almost every smart phone has a step counter on it now or you can get those fancy wrist computers to do it. Challenge yourself to beat your daily average or all-time record.

Chapter 21
Water Thyself

I wish I could take my own advice when it comes to water. It is so good for you. The average adult should be drinking at least eight glasses a day. Organizations like Weight Watchers teach this before you even walk in the door.

Without proper hydration, your body gets tired and wrinkled and holds onto water like it will never see another drop. Just look at me! Most of us need to drink a lot more water.

I am getting better. The one trick I have adopted that works well is to have water handy at all times. I have a case of bottled water in my bedroom closet so I can drink a bottle as soon as I wake up in the morning. This gets your metabolism going and kick-starts your day. I have a water bottle in my office that I can fill up at the office cooler to keep within arm's reach as I work. If it's in front of me, I drink it. I drink water at restaurants if it is put in front of me, yet forget to ask for it if it is not.

Make it simple for yourself and drink water. Your body will thank you.

Chapter 22
Wash Your Hands

My daughters are tired of me telling them to wash their hands before cooking, eating or empting the dishwasher. And after using the bathroom! Obviously repetition does not work for this attempted education. Washing one's hands is one of the best ways to stay healthy and avoid spreading germs. I recently heard it said that if everyone in the world washed their hands properly, a million lives could be saved a year!

When you cannot wash your hands regularly, keep them away from your face in order to avoid spreading germs to the most susceptible places like your eyes, nose and ears. Use your towel, a sleeve or a shoulder to open doors in public places. I know it sounds a bit over-the-top, but why do you want all those other people's germs on your hands?

Chapter 23
Stop the Salt

There was a time when I really didn't pay attention or care about sodium. Salt. White death. I have never been one to add salt to my food or even to my cooking, unlike my former father-in-law that would shake the salt over his entire meal before even tasting it. But I used to love those Asian noodle packages that you boil in water and add the little packets of flavour and dehydrated vegetable pieces. Or at least I hope that's what they were. Then I started reading the nutrition information labels and saw they have 1,800 or more grams of sodium in a single serving. Yikes.

I have since learned most of the sodium we consume comes from the prepared foods we eat like those noodles and not the salt we sprinkle on our foods at the table. Sodium is added to packaged food by the manufacturers to make foods taste better and as consumers we have become very used to it. Maybe we're even addicted. When we eat foods with little or no sodium, we may think it lacks flavour.

Why is that so bad? Too much sodium in your system causes your body to retain water. This is hard on your heart and blood vessels. Some people get high blood pressure. The Heart and Stroke Foundation says our bodies only need 200 mg of sodium per day to do its business of helping to balance fluids and electrolytes in our bodies. That's about one-twelfth of a teaspoon of salt. They also say your target should be no more than 2,300 mg or the equivalent of one teaspoon of salt.

So avoid adding table salt to your food. Most recipes that call for salt don't need it, unless you are baking something complicated that requires it for a chemical reaction. I even started checking the canned soda water we were buying – what could be better for you than carbonated water? But I found some of them have really high sodium levels.

It doesn't do any good to say, "I don't add any salt to my food". You don't have to add it – it's already in there. Read the labels and choose foods that are low in sodium or have "no salt added" on the label.

Chapter 24
To Throw or Not to Throw

Refrigerators are a very personal thing. You can tell a lot about someone by peering into their private little hideaway of coldness.

My friend Sheri's fridge is packed absolutely solid, like some elaborate game of Jenga. If you cook with her, you need to be medicated if she asks you to "just grab the hot sauce" as you hope you don't destroy the eco system removing and replacing items. It never quite fits the same way as she had it in there.

In my short-lived bachelor days, my fridge was the exact opposite of Sheri's. It had ketchup, mustard, beer, cola, milk and butter in it. I ate out at restaurants all the time and if I did eat at home it consisted of a large bowl of popcorn. That explains the butter.

My former in-laws' fridge was full of hundreds of containers of leftover bits and pieces from meals and recipes gone by. I suspect this was a result of growing up without much money and cherishing every piece of food. This prompted my former father-in-law to often proclaim, "Is it worth dying over?" when his wife would offer up some ancient morsel they had saved for a later date.

So besides the psychological interest of comparing fridge contents with people's lifestyle or personality, it pays to know a few rules about refrigerator safety. Generally, things should not be consumed after 2-3 days in the fridge after they were originally prepared. This is especially true for things containing eggs, dairy products or mayonnaise. Fresh meats will only be safe 3-5 days after purchase, except poultry which should be cooked in 1-2 days. If something is frozen and gets thawed, do not re-freeze it.

"Best before" and "use by" dates are another mystery, since a study recently proclaimed North Americans throw out $165 billion dollars' worth of edible food every year because of the labels. Use some common sense here and assume a few days past the date is fine and two years past is not.

Oh, and the great idea of putting beer in the freezer to get cold? This turns into a really bad idea and a huge mess when you forget about it.

Chapter 25
The Early Bird

I would never claim I am a morning person, early-riser or otherwise. There is nothing on this earth I would rather do than to roll over and go back to sleep. But I have learned to set the alarm a little bit earlier to achieve so much more in my day. Writers and scholars long before me have been saying that in order to get a different result from everyone else on this planet, you have to do something different than everyone else.

Getting up 30 minutes earlier changes my day, my health and my mood. It gives me time to exercise, prepare a decent breakfast, make sure I have a homemade lunch packed and be ahead of the worst traffic for my commute. Before I did this, I would have never believed that rising just a little bit sooner could make such a difference.

The other serendipity to my earliness is being one of the first people in the office each morning. It has an incredible calming effect because it puts you ahead instead of behind right from the start. And I'll bet you can guess who the guy is that is one of the first people to leave the office each day.

Chapter 26
Sleep Soundly

My mom was a miracle of survival on very little sleep. Or at least it seemed that way to her family. She would sit up late at night pouring over the family budget, reading novels and watching every crime show on television. Then she would be up again long before the rest of us preparing a hot breakfast and getting bagged lunches ready. I never knew how she did it, especially since I have already mentioned my affinity for sleeping.

But there is no need to take my word for the value of sleep, since most doctors and many medical journals speak of its value. And don't forget that mind-boggling statistic about how we spend one-third of our lives in bed. That's based on eight hours of sleep each night.

The challenge, however, is that many of us do not get enough sleep. Certainly I was guilty of this in my younger days of late-night studying, socializing and later on being up at all hours with young children. I simply can't function on less than eight hours now and make sure that my life and social plans allow for this.

Sleep rejuvenates brain cells, heals the body and reduces anxiety. If you ever have to wonder how important it is, think about how you feel the week after you set the clocks ahead for daylight savings time and lose that hour. There are more accidents and illness in that week than in any other the whole year long!

You can also improve the quality and duration of your sleep by making some changes to your sleeping environment. Ensure it is dark enough – we used to put aluminum foil on my daughters' bedroom windows to make it totally dark, especially when bedtime was before sunset. Get the temperature right – we like it cold in the room with a big fluffy duvet to keep us warm. And try not to eat or drink within a few hours of bedtime so your stomach is done all its work before you lay down.

Be Nice

Chapter 27
Walk the Talk

An old Native American proverb states to not judge a man until you have walked a mile in his shoes. This quote has been rephrased and repeated many times in songs and movies, but bears repeating in a specific context. I think this advice applies even more to people not walking in shoes, like those in casts or wheelchairs.

My partner broke a foot recently and was in a series of fiberglass casts for many weeks and walking precariously on crutches. It was an eye-opening experience for both of us to watch how people did not allow extra room, open doors or offer any kind of assistance. One little girl ran past us on a narrow sidewalk and kicked the crutches, but the real surprise was how her parents looked at us as if we had done something wrong.

Even when we were using a wheelchair at the airport or in shopping malls, it was shocking to us how few people would allow extra room or offer assistance as we struggled with luggage or packages and through non-accessible doorways.

So, imagine yourself walking a mile in someone else's cast – maybe even on icy sidewalks with crutches that were designed in the dark ages. And then be extra kind!

Chapter 28
Just Say Thank You

It might sound like basic kindergarten logic, but two of the most important words in your vocabulary are "thank you." Often those two words are all that is required, even when you might be tempted to write an epistle of gratitude.

The same applies when someone gives you a compliment on your outfit, your house or the work you just completed. Just say, "thank you" and leave it at that. Many of us are compelled to respond to praise with long explanations of how "it was nothing" and this only serves to make the other person wish they had not bothered.

Chapter 29
Say it Safely

Most of us have heard the old line, "If you don't have something nice to say, don't say anything at all." Besides being a cliché comment from parents to children, this statement is really good advice and should be applied often.

A work colleague of mine many years ago would almost always respond to a new mother's announcement of her pregnancy by asking, "Was it planned?" I really never figured out the expected response to that.

When my partner had a broken foot and met new people while wearing the cast or protective boot, people would often respond to, "How are you?" with, "Better than you obviously."

I have also learned to never ever suggest or ask if a woman is expecting a baby unless you actually see the baby coming out of her. It's just a bad idea to make that assumption without knowing for sure.

Like so many things, the best response may be to take your parents advice and just smile, say nothing or have a short polite reply ready when you think you might say something dumb.

Chapter 30
Get Good at Being a Guest

Have you ever been a server or a bus person in a restaurant or a banquet facility? My career as a bus person at Capri Pizza when I was 13 years old lasted for exactly one night. They made me work until 2:00 in the morning and did not drive me home. My dad went to the restaurant the next day and told them a few things, including that I would not be back.

Both of my daughters have had part-time jobs as servers and have made good money and good friends. More importantly, I think this is a job that every one of us should do at one time in our lives so we learn to be good at being a guest.

The rules apply equally in a restaurant and in your own or someone else's home. When you leave the table for good or just to go the washroom, push your chair in. Nobody wants to walk around it or trip over it. When you are finished your meal, place your silverware neatly across the middle of the plate, firstly as a signal that you are done eating and also so they do not fall off when the plate is cleared. There is nothing worse than a fork and knife hanging like oars off your plate so that the server or host has to move them or risk dropping them on you or someone else.

This is a good time to remember your manners and say please and thank-you often. The server or your host is working hard to create a great experience for you and deserves some positive feedback!

Chapter 31
Forever Flatter

I am not sure who first coined the phrase, "flattery will get you nowhere," but I believe in the opposite.

Every single person in this world wants to be noticed and appreciated. Dale Carnegie taught, "A person's name is to him or her the sweetest and most important sound in any language." So you can actually show appreciation to someone just by the fact you remembered their name.

Giving honest and sincere acknowledgement to another person does not need to be shallow or fake either. You just need to get good at noticing little details like a new haircut, dress or shirt on another person and adding the word "nice" in front of it and their name after it.

If you want to take this a step further, try complimenting the person rather than the item by saying, "You look great in that haircut/dress/shirt." Pretty simple advice that can make the other person's day a lot brighter and thinking you are the kindest person they know.

Chapter 32
Shake a Paw

Greetings are not universal, but in most of the countries to which I have traveled a warm handshake is a very acceptable gesture. Try to be the first to extend your hand, whether it is to a long-time friend or a stranger. And learn to be good at it!

One "shake" with a small amount of pressure is the way to go. Never squeeze someone's hand hard, but rather just be firm. The opposite is just as bad, so don't be a limp fish with a handshake that has no substance behind it.

One should always stand to shake another person's hand if seated and look them in the eye while doing it. A trick I learned for a situation where you might be wearing a name tag is to wear it on your right chest so it "turns" toward the person as you extend your right hand to them.

Chapter 33
Name of the Game

As previously noted, Dale Carnegie was among many who have extolled the virtues of remembering a person's name. This is one of the most essential elements of customer service and also of common decency. I will put my hand in the air as having always struggled with this skill. But there are tips and tricks you can put into action to make you better at this.

First of all, always give your name first when you meet someone new (as you are giving them a nice firm handshake). When they return the favour and give you their name, repeat it to them with a "Nice to meet you, Joe." By saying it out loud it will register better in your brain. Use a person's name as often as possible in conversation and remember it for the next time. I will venture a guess that you always feel better patronizing a business where they remember your name?

There are all sorts of tricks to remember names too. Jot it down in a notebook or put it in your phone. You can also try using fun clues to remember a name like, "Her name is Penny. Like a shiny penny. I always get the correct change from her."

Chapter 34
Stand and Smile

One of the interesting things about technology is how it is changing the world around us and how we act. I often find it amusing to watch people do the cell phone shuffle, as I call it. Watch most people take a call in a public place and they will pace and scurry to find a quiet and private place to talk. What is equally amusing about this is I was always taught to stand and smile before answering the phone. It makes you sound happy and interested on the other end!

So whether you are taking a call in your office, at home or in a crowded restaurant, stand and smile before you say hello.

Chapter 35
Show Your Hand

Growing up in a big city as I did, I was not too familiar with the custom of waving at people I did not know well. When my older sister moved to a ranch after marriage, I was very surprised the first time a complete stranger waved as they passed us on a country road. "Who was that?" I would ask and usually get in response, "Probably a neighbour." Probably?

I learned that people in small towns and communities wave at everyone because it's the neighbourly thing to do. Shouldn't we all be like this?

Try it out and enjoy the results. Wave at children on a school bus as it passes. Wave at people as they drive past your home. Nod your head or wave at the elderly pedestrian taking a few extra seconds to cross the road in front of your car – and when someone stops for you to cross the road.

Chapter 36
Acknowledge the Anthem

When I managed a large hosting facility at a major sporting event, one of my colleagues would never stop talking during the national anthem. I cannot think of anything more disrespectful. Especially when all of the guests and serving staff had risen and stopped talking and he was the only person speaking!

It might seem like old-school manners, but I believe it is one of the times that tradition should endure. Stop dead in your tracks, stand if seated, take off your hat and discontinue speaking (unless you are singing along). You will be back to your food, beverage and friends in just a few seconds and your country will appreciate the respect.

Chapter 37
Reward with Respect

It still surprises me when you ask a young child what they want to "be" when they grow up and the answer is very often something like a firefighter, police officer or doctor. My response was always that I wanted to be a teacher. We look up to certain professions because they are serving such an important role and often something not all of us can or would want to do.

Everyone on this earth deserves respect and kindness. But there are also certain people who warrant a special mention in this category and they seem to parallel those "what I want to be" categories.

So show the utmost of respect to teachers, clergy, firefighters, police officers, doctors and nurses. They often encounter us at our worst possible moments and, although they are trained to deal with it, do not ever deserve to be treated poorly by us. Show this same respect whether you are young and they are old and vice versa.

And don't forget the server at the coffee shop or the cashier at the grocery store. They are serving us to make our day better and deserve as much respect as the Queen of England!

Chapter 38
Travel Teaches

Someone very wise once said travel is the only thing you buy that makes you richer. It is hard to grasp this concept until you actually are lucky enough to travel, but I cannot agree more.

It is incredibly humbling to see other places and cultures and witness how they do things so differently. It teaches us above all else that we do not always have all the answers. To see how others work, eat, live and love is the greatest teacher in the world.

One of my favourite things to do in a place I am visiting is to go to the grocery store. I find it fascinating to see the different products not available in my home town and read labels in different languages. I also love comparing prices and either counting myself very lucky or very unlucky for what I pay for a similar item at home!

Travel does not have to be over a continent or ocean to get the benefits. Even the next town or province has different ways of living and can be a brand new experience for us.

Chapter 39
Listen to Learn

I was taught at a young age to be silent unless I had something worthwhile to share or, in other words, speak when I was spoken to. I was already quite a shy person and this was not a difficult task for me!

As I matured, went to school, earned a university degree and got my first job I learned the value of this advice. I also had to learn when to speak up and express my opinion and when a contribution to a discussion would benefit everyone. Sometimes it's a difficult balance.

Something worthwhile to remember is that we have two ears, two eyes and one mouth for a reason. There is nothing worse than someone that does not listen to instructions or the knowledge of others and then asks dumb questions. Or someone that ignores signs or written instructions and complains they were misinformed.

Chapter 40
Front Fascinates

If you want to stand out in this world, there is nothing easier to do than to just let other people ahead of you. I'm not talking about being a doormat and letting people walk all over you – figuratively or actually. I am referring to a common courtesy that is just not that common anymore.

When approaching or passing through a doorway, hold the door open for someone else. When stepping onto or off an elevator, let the other people go first. In traffic, let that person ahead of you into your lane ahead of you. At the grocery store, let the person with a handful of items ahead of you.

The reward is knowing you have done something very few others will and you will likely get a smile and a heartfelt thank you in return. Nobody gets too many of those in their day. And you will get to where you are going only seconds behind where you would have otherwise.

Be Social

Chapter 41
Watch Your Words

It used to be that you could only put your foot in your mouth by actually speaking something rude, dumb or inappropriate directly to another person. You could of course have taken out a pen or a typewriter and written a regrettable note to someone, but there were likely too many opportunities to catch yourself before you sent it and you likely ripped it up. I am a master of "the letter" and wish I would have stopped before sending a few in my past.

With the advent of email, text messages and social media everything is now instant, including saying things you might regret later. My rule here – and what I have always told my daughters – is to not put anything in an email, text or online unless you would say the exact same thing in a crowded elevator. It lives forever and can instantly be re-sent around the world!

A former boss of mine was a master of the 24-hour rule and taught me well to use it. It involves going ahead and writing the letter, email, text or online post and then not sending it for 24 hours if it could at all be upsetting or misinterpreted by the recipient. Tuck it away and save it as a draft until tomorrow. You will find that more times than not you will delete it when you read it again in the light of a new day. In the interim, you will have expressed your feelings on paper and "gotten it off your chest" as they say. Often that is enough to erase it from your thoughts and move on with a new day.

Chapter 42
Don't Mix

If you enjoy alcoholic beverages – and I am certainly not here to judge anyone either way – you have likely overindulged at some point in your life. If you have not, good for you!

My least favourite story on this subject involves a 19-year old version of me attending a party to which I brought a warm box of white wine. Yes, you read that correctly – a box. Because the wine was warm, we placed it in the freezer to chill and proceeded to have some other mixed cocktails and a few shooters to pass the time until the wine was ready to enjoy. I cannot remember ever being in more physical pain than I was later that evening and the next day.

When partaking in alcoholic beverages, one should never ever mix except in a few proven cases. So remember this little ditty. Liquor before beer, in the clear; beer before liquor, never been sicker. I am sure there are other proven tricks, but this one has served me well, especially now that I purchase my beverages in bottles rather than boxes.

Chapter 43
Hangovers Hurt

Before you crash for the night after over-indulging, pour yourself a glass of chocolate milk and take the maximum dose of ibuprofen. It sounds odd, but it has been working like a charm for me for many years.

Chocolate milk is also a great alternative to cough medicine. Imagine that?

Chapter 44
Gorgeous Gifts

I have my sister Judy to thank for teaching me how to properly and beautifully wrap a gift. I take a lot of time to find the right size box, to ensure the correct placement of the gift inside with copious amounts of tissue paper and carefully select the paper, ribbon, bow and tags for the outside. Wrapping Christmas gifts is a weekend-long event for me, but there is nothing more satisfying than a stack of beautifully wrapped gifts. Yes, I'm weird.

Gift bags are easy to get and cheap to buy. Of course I have been guilty of buying a last-minute gift and tossing it into a gift bag in the back seat of the car right after I signed the card on the dashboard! As a rule, however, I prefer to tell the person for whom the gift is intended that I spent some time finding the gift and put some care into its packaging.

Chapter 45
Tables Tell Tales

I am constantly amazed at how many people do not know how to set a table properly and even more surprised at people who do not know which piece of tableware to use when they are the guest. It is even more amazing when it is my own family members who have been shown a few hundred times!

It doesn't need to be complicated at all. Silverware is set around the plate in the order it is to be used. If you are starting with a salad before the main entrée, the salad fork – usually smaller – goes on the outside of the larger fork on the left side of the plate. Similarly, a spoon for soup to be served before the entrée should go on the outside of the knife on the right side of the plate. This is also where you would place a spoon for twirling your pasta. If your appetizer requires a knife, place it on the outside also so it gets used first. Forks or spoons for dessert and coffee are best set at the top of the plate. That way they are all that is left when your plate is removed after the main course.

Which glass and plate are mine? Any side plate for bread or buns should be immediately at your left. Your glassware is at the top of your dinner knife on the right hand side. Keep your hands off other guests stuff!

When you are the guest and sit down to a properly set table, it is very easy to know what utensil, plate or glass to use and it even gives you a sneak peek into what is going to be served. Always start from the outside and work your way to the inside and you will be the expert at the table!

Chapter 46
Be a Host with the Most

For the longest time, I always joked about what was the ultimate thing to serve at a dinner party. It was Pheasant Under Glass. La tee dah. I have never made it and it's probably not that great.

I think I must have learned this from a Saturday-morning cartoon as a little kid. There was an old *Foghorn Leghorn* cartoon where Foghorn fools the little chicken hawk into thinking he has painted him invisible and sends him after "Pheasant Under Glass", which is actually the barnyard dog. It's odd what sticks with you from your childhood. But I digress.

My point here is to be a good host and throw great parties. You don't need to spend a lot of money to take it up a notch from bags of potato chips or store-bought hors d'oeuvres that are full of salt and scary preservatives.

Cut cheese into little rectangle blocks and wrap a piece of cold meat around them (prosciutto is nice) – then secure it with a toothpick. Heat up some meatballs and douse them with a nice barbecue sauce or a mixture of cranberry sauce and a spicy hot sauce. Tuck wonton wrappers into a buttered muffin tin and fill with chopped crab, chicken, tuna or ham mixed with some mayonnaise, cheese and spices and then bake them.

Remember the real reason you have invited people over to your home is to have some fun and socialize. You don't want to be in the kitchen all night preparing things and you also don't want your guests suggesting you order a pizza because they are starving. It's a fine line. With a little planning, you can learn to be great at walking it.

Chapter 47
Holiday Cards

When I was a kid, my parents would spend hours and even days writing personal notes in beautiful Christmas cards. My mom always liked ones with Currier and Ives scenes on the front and very traditional greetings inside. When I was old enough to send my own cards, I chose silly cards with *Ziggy* and funny Santas on them. Each envelope was carefully addressed on the typewriter, the information taken from elaborate journals that kept track of who had sent cards to us in previous years. The rule of thumb was that if you didn't get a card back for a few years in a row, you were off the list. Harsh!

The message here is that it is still appropriate and very nice to take the time once a year to put down the mouse or smartphone and send a personal greeting to your friends and family in a real envelope with a real stamp. Include a recent photo of you and your family, if you have one, and you have made a wonderful gesture without hardly any technology involved. It doesn't even have to be at the holidays. Maybe your thing is to send out a card for everyone's birthday or send out New Year's or Fourth of July cards.

Chapter 48
Preserve the Past

One of my favourite things to do at my parents' house was to go through old photo albums and musty boxes of photographs that had never really been organized. It was fun to see people I knew – and a lot that I didn't – in different fashions, hairstyles and times.

I worry that current and future generations may be at risk of losing all photographic record of their existence. It sounds a bit drastic until you really think about it for a moment. All the "old" photos we enjoy now are in printed form and are hiding in museums, boxes, photo albums and archives. If an old photo is available electronically, it was probably scanned from a hard copy. But right now most of us keep our current photos on our phones and computers.

Ever try to access a file or photo you saved on a floppy disc a dozen years ago? They don't exist anymore and therefore no computer can read it. Think all your photos are safe because you have them on your computer and backed up on the cloud or a jump drive? Think about what happens as the technology changes as it does every day.

I am a perfect example of this and suspect I am not alone. I have dozens of photo albums of my children up until the day I bought a digital camera and a smart phone. The albums stop abruptly. I have newer photos on screensavers and in electronic albums, but I am fearful of what will happen if I don't keep "moving" them to the latest platform.

My advice here is to print off as many favourite photos as you can and organize them somewhere that is not dependent on any technology other than your eyes. You can pull them out for grandchildren without the need for electronics and enjoy again a bit of your past.

Chapter 49
Awesome Answers

My dear friend and colleague Kelly has the most amazing list of questions she uses in job interviews. They are not at all traditional and the farthest thing from, "Tell me a little bit about yourself." I have borrowed them often for both interviews and social gatherings to take the conversation in a new direction!

From over 100, here are some of my favourites:

Just entertain me for five minutes. I'm not going to talk.

What do you think of garden gnomes?

If you could be any character in fiction, who would you be?

Would you be willing to put together an IKEA bookshelf?

Do you have good manners?

What was the last thing you downloaded?

Do you have a lucky number, shirt, rock…?

Sell me this.

The point here is the answers are not really that important! It is how the other person reacts to talking about seemingly unimportant things and "thinks on their feet." In social gatherings, it's fun to use this type of question to get the topic off the weather and what you are making for dinner. You can make up your own and have a little fun!

Chapter 50
Beautiful Birthdays

Just as a person's name is the most cherished word they long to hear, a birthday is the most important day of the year and deserves to be recognized. My partner often tells the story of riding a bicycle to the grocery store to pick up a birthday cake for their own celebration when the family forgot to plan ahead. Not fun.

These days there is social media to 'bing and bong' to tell us, "Today is so-and-so's birthday," but I recommend going beyond a simple text or post to really make the birthday-person's day. Why not send or give a greeting card like the good old days? Bake some cookies and leave them on their doorstep. Or maybe a bottle of wine will fit the bill. A cake always says it best.

A birthday is the one occasion during the year that person shares with no one else (except about 1/365th of the world) and they deserve to get all the attention. Unless you are my daughter and son-in-law who share a birthday. But they get double the fun!

Chapter 51
Humble Holidays

Depending on the country you live in, there are dozens of national holidays each year on the calendar. For some of the occasions, offices and shops are closed and workers get a day off work or long weekend.

Whatever your plans on these special days, it's worthwhile to take a moment to remember the reason the day was designated in the first place. Whether it's to honour war veterans or celebrate the life of a noteworthy leader or monarch, consider reading a bit about that person or piece of history and even participating in a commemorative event in your community. It never hurts to learn a little bit more about your country's past.

Chapter 52
Unplug to Unwind

Technology is a wonderful thing and I am certainly not one of those people to condemn it as evil. Our little devices that have become such a part of our lives do save us time and allow us to communicate so much faster than ever before. I would be the first to admit I am lost if I forget my phone in another place or even another room!

But, as with much in life, there is always the chance of too much of a good thing. When computers with their keyboards and mice became commonplace, we soon had carpal tunnel syndrome in wrists from overuse. Now we hear about afflictions like enlarged thumbs on our youth from too much texting or gaming and, more recently, something called 'text neck' from the odd position in which we put ourselves while staring at our devices.

Many people 'plug in' with ear buds to listen to music on their devices. Almost everyone I pass on my lunchtime walk has wires dangling from their ears. What happened to listening to the birds sing or the wind in the trees?

My partner and I love to go on cruise vacations and one of the odd serendipities of this form of travel is that the internet and wireless connections are usually terrible or very expensive. It's a great excuse to put our phones and other devices in the safe and never use them for the duration of the cruise. It makes for an 'unplugged" vacation experience and is incredibly refreshing.

Stepping away from our technology for short bursts is very hard at first. Some families have rules about no devices at the dinner table or after certain times of the day. That's a great place to start. I hope we never get to a place where a good conversation with a smile and some eye contact is completely forgotten and replaced with technology.

Give it a try. Make up your own 'no screen time' moments and see if the world stops turning. I am guessing you will be surprised and enjoy it.

Chapter 53
Play Perfectly

As a young man, I was lucky enough to be part of the school band and, later on, a city-wide marching band. It was not only a fantastic opportunity to learn to play an instrument, but also a chance to travel to places I had never visited.

One of the things you learn very quickly in a band or orchestra is everyone has their own part to play in the tune. All players have a unique piece of music in front of them. The trumpets do not play the flute part. The drums do not play the trombone music. And vice versa all around. Without each person playing the correct notes at the correct time, the whole thing falls apart and sounds awful.

I am not sure who first said it, but there is an old adage that says something like, "There is your business and there is none of your business." You have your music to play and the other person has theirs. This parallels life in general as we are all born to do different things and live our lives in different ways.

It helps to remember the orchestra when we are tempted to control someone else's behaviour or, worse yet, letting their behaviour control ours or the way we feel. Being in charge of only our own notes in the tune is a great lesson for us to learn.

Be Safe

Chapter 54
Wipers On, Lights On

I am not sure where I learned it, but it must have been in some secret club since I rarely see it in practice. Quite simply, if your windshield wipers are on to remove rain, sleet or snow from your windshield then your head lights should also be on.

The logic in this comes from the fact that the rain, sleet or snow is coming from clouds above that are also blocking the sun and making it darker outside. And if everyone else is also driving while trying to remove wetness from in front of their vision, it makes great sense to help them see you clearly by turning on your lights.

Chapter 55
Parking or Passing

Many new cars now are equipped with automatic sensors to turn on your headlights, but some common sense still applies. That is why there is still always a way for you to manually control them.

First of all, parking lights are for... parking! This is usually the first "click" when you turn on your lights and it just turns on the little orange or white front lights of your car and not the headlights or tail lights. These lights are not intended for driving and were designed to use minimal power when your car is not running. When you are driving, your car's alternator makes the electricity for your head lights to burn brightly.

Be safe and put ALL your lights on when it is necessary. Unless you are actually parked.

Chapter 56
Signal for Safety

The modern turn signal was apparently patented around 1938 and subsequently offered by most major automobile manufacturers. Before that, a system of hand signals were used such as is still used on bicycles. Given that history, you would expect more drivers to actually use this little gadget.

Even though you have driven the same route every day and know that you are turning at that corner up ahead, the other drivers do not. When you suddenly change lanes or turn a corner without notifying the other drivers and pedestrians, you make it very dangerous for everyone.

Another lesson I was taught in driver training was to always use your turn signal before you press the brake pedal. That way everyone knows why you are braking because they have already been notified of your desire to make a turn ahead. Brilliant!

Another thing worth remembering is using the signal light does not make your vehicle turn the corner. You still have to follow the rules of the road and steer your car. Don't flick on your signal light and expect everyone else to move out of your way just because you have announced your intentions.

Chapter 57
Stride Safe

My advice on being a safe pedestrian is similar to my advice when you're in a vehicle or on a bicycle. Don't assume everyone else knows your intentions.

My least favourite habit of hurrying walkers is when they stand at a corner with their toes hanging over the edge of the curb. This isn't an Olympic sprinting event. You are just making all the drivers nervous that you are going to suddenly fall into traffic and be smooshed – that's the technical term.

Besides being illegal, jaywalking is really dangerous. Cross at the corner just like your mother taught you and not when the signal says not to – especially in front of a train.

Chapter 58
Guards for the Grass

High on the list of things that make me wince and run for cover is witnessing someone cutting their grass or trimming the edges in flip-flops and with no eye protection. Even worse is when they have their little children and pets out there with them! I am wincing right now as I write this.

We are all guilty of doing jobs around the house without full personal protective equipment, but this one is common sense. Lawn mowers and grass trimmers are really sharp and also throw at high speed things like rocks and other debris that might be hiding in your grass. Cover your toes with shoes and your eyes with sunglasses or protective lenses – and save the gardening lesson for junior until after the dangerous stuff is over.

Chapter 59
Biking Basics

When I was a young child, there was a campaign to "share the road" to encourage bicycles and vehicles to co-exist on the city's streets. I am quite sure there have been many similar initiatives over the years, but once again, common sense seems to have gone out the window.

Are you a bike, a vehicle or a pedestrian? Logic says that you cannot be more than one at the same time.

Almost every day I see bikers whiz between cars, through stop signs and red lights without even pausing and, my favourite, riding across the road in a pedestrian crosswalk. The worst is when I see parents riding with small children and performing these same stunts.

Riding a bike is great exercise, but comes with responsibilities. My advice is to follow the rules of the road or get off the road and stick to a bike path. It will be safer for everyone.

Chapter 60
Laws Lead

Driving a car in a busy city is an educational experience. I seem to be one of the few that drives the speed limit, stops at red lights and does not follow the vehicle in front of me too close. No, I am not perfect. But I believe in obeying the laws and driving like I would if there was a police car right beside me. I believe in the principal of doing the right thing even if I think nobody is watching.

Someone smarter than me decided on the speed limits for the roads I use and put up traffic lights at intersections that require controlling. Breaking those rules and laws makes you a criminal, even if you think nobody is watching or the rule is just a suggestion.

The laws are there first and foremost for our safety and I am unclear why people in vehicles believe they are somehow immune as they hurtle forward in thousands of pounds of metal with only a painted line separating them from the people doing the same thing in the opposite direction!

You had to learn the rules and laws when you studying and were tested for your driver's license, so why not follow them and do everyone a favour?

Be Frugal

Chapter 61
Happy Hotels

Travelling with my friend Gail gave me new appreciation for taking control of the situation as a paying guest. As soon as she would enter a hotel room, Gail would immediately flush the toilet and make sure it worked well. There is nothing worse or more embarrassing, she said, than having to call the front desk to request a maintenance person to come and take a plunger to a full bowl. The very first time I took Gail's advice, the "test" flush flooded the entire bathroom and I was a very pleased person to not have unpacked yet!

Never accept a room with a door to an adjoining room unless you are also occupying that room with other members of your family or group. You will hear every sound from the other room and so will they!

Most hotel websites have a place to indicate your preferences when you reserve a room. Rooms reserved on the telephone always have a reservation agent eager to jot down these notes as well. Take advantage of this by being specific that you want a room far away or close to the elevator or on a high or low floor. And be sure to check that your preferences have been considered when you get your room key at check in!

Chapter 62
Shop Sales

Call me cheap or call me frugal, but I am a sale shopper and proud of it. I am not a fanatic that clips enough coupons to get their entire grocery order for free or anything like those shows on television. I simply refuse to pay regular price.

My daughters can attest that, as of a very young age, they knew to not put anything in the grocery cart unless it was on sale. This, of course, tended to backfire as they ran around the store finding all the candy and potato chips that were on sale and bringing them to the cart. Not exactly what I had in mind.

In general, if it's not available at a sale price, I don't buy it. Not then anyway. I wait a week, a month or a year until it is offered at a better price. And it almost always is. If you follow the grocery store flyers you know that bathroom tissue is on sale every second or third week. Why would you buy it on the off weeks then? Certain fresh meats are also on sale in cycles. Almost everything is. It takes a little planning to stock up when it's on sale and walk past when it is not.

My reward is the money saved and the little surprised announcement by the cashier at the exit with their, "Oh! You saved $57 today."

Clothing works the same for me. I know that the winter stuff will be on sale at or around Christmas to make way for the spring stuff. And the summer stuff is on sale practically before the summer even gets started – at least a Canadian summer anyway. No self-respecting retailer ever puts its sale racks at the front of the store. That spot is saved for all the swanky new styles and colours. Walk directly to the very back corners and there you will find the on-sale treasures.

Chapter 63
Recycle and Re-Do

Recycling usually involves finding a new use for trash or things you no longer need that can be used by others, but you can recycle within your own home to save money too. My partner happens to be the world-champion on watching the same movie or television series over and over. Together, we have watched every episode of the Golden Girls at least a dozen times!

If you have a favourite movie or book that brought you joy and entertainment the first time, why not watch or read it again? Chances are you missed a few details the first time anyway. Flip through that stack of old magazines. Go through those old cookbooks. Play a board game you have not opened in ages.

And the best form of recycling is exchanging your favourite books and discs with friends. Although I do caution you on lending your true favourites if you are not absolutely sure you will see them again.

Chapter 64
Magazine Mayhem

I am one of those people who doesn't really enjoy reading books, magazines or news online. There is something about holding a printed and bound document in my hands. I guess I am old-fashioned that way.

Quite recently I discovered you can get some really great deals on subscriptions to magazines sent to your home. They are usually more than 50 percent cheaper than buying them at a store and you get every issue. I now have subscriptions to several magazines and enjoy them immensely for pennies a day.

The other thing I had to learn late in life is that a magazine I have purchased is really mine to use however I wish. I was brought up to treasure such things and put them back on the bookshelf where one found them in nice neat stacks.

With this in mind, you can feel free to rip out that great recipe you see, let the kids cut them up for a school project and pin ads for your dream car up on the fridge or bulletin board. A new puppy or bird? Well, that use is really up to you. It's really very economical entertainment.

Chapter 65
House Brands Help

It's not news to anyone that when you visit the grocery store or pharmacy you will find many different brands of the same product. And because of the great influence of marketing, our eyes and minds are naturally drawn to the brands we have seen on billboards, in magazines, on television and online.

But one of the choices for most common products is the house brand. It might carry the same name of the store or some other catchy name, but you can figure it out pretty quick when there is that version of almost every product at your store.

In almost all cases, these products are made by the same famous manufacturers as the ones you have seen advertised. The store does not have its own ketchup, chocolate, aspirin or pasta factory. But there are no marketing dollars or fancy packaging costs being spent on these products and they are almost always cheaper. Try them out and save some money!

Chapter 66
Homemade Hilarity

I will sound like a really old person on this piece of advice, but I believe it gets forgotten in our modern world of technology and "screen" entertainment. The best fun does not have to cost anything at all.

If it's summer and you're warm, put on your swimsuit and run through the garden sprinkler. If it's winter and there is snow, bundle up and build a big snowman. Rake some leaves and jump in them. Sit outside and watch a sunrise or sunset. Play a card game with yourself, friends or family. Go for a long walk. The list is really endless and the budget is very tiny.

Chapter 67
Fricking Frugal

One of my favourite episodes of the classic sitcom The Golden Girls features Rose being frustrated by her boyfriend Miles and how tight he is with money. He often uses coupons for their dinner dates and in frustration Rose calls him, "Fricking frugal."

My partner and I have been accused of being overly frugal sometimes. When we sit down at a restaurant and look at the menu, we both gravitate to the cheapest items on the menu and sometimes have to catch each other. I guess we see the big picture that saving on some things means you can splurge on others. Travelling happens to be an area where we are not that frugal!

My advice here is to balance your frugality with the odd decadence. Life is too short to try to save your way to riches. Life is about celebrating along the way and not waiting for some future perfect picture. Every apparent overnight success has taken many years to get there.

Be Organized

Chapter 68
Be the First

Monikers like teacher's pet or brown-noser are the negative views of being polite to one's superiors. Take the positive approach and be rewarded!

When something is due to your teacher, professor or boss, be the first one to hand it in. This is one area where it pays to win the race. Do it often and you will be remembered for being the first, even if your submission is not perfect.

In my experience as both a boss and a subordinate, no one wants to spend time reminding people over and over to hand something in. But a quick response is always appreciated and remembered. In the new millennium, this goes for responding to emails also. Even if you don't have the exact or immediate answer to someone's question or enquiry, responding quickly with, "I will check and get right back to you," will win you points every time.

Chapter 69
Prepare Properly

I wish I was one of those people who can go through life seemingly oblivious to rules and accepted ways of doing things. It's not that I am recommending this approach. It just fascinates me and is so opposite to the way I am.

Take our recent trip overseas for a long-awaited vacation. I researched every rule from the allowable size of the hand luggage to the procedure for connecting to another airline in London. Then I watched mature people – who I really have to guess have flown on an airplane before in the recent past – try to bring full-size toiletries through security. And do not have their photo identification out for boarding the plane despite at least five reminder announcements from the customer service agent at the gate. Or ring the flight attendant during boarding to get a bite to eat when the poor crew is just trying to get the airplane door shut.

My advice here is to be prepared. Like a Boy Scout. There is an absolute excess of information waiting for you in libraries and online if you take a little time to look for it. Don't be the one holding up the line or abusing the system because you're out of the loop.

Chapter 70
Neat Is Nice

I have recently read some studies that suggest a messy desk or work space is a sign of a creative mind. Although I do not have any scientific facts to back me up, I beg to differ.

I may be on the extreme end of this debate, but I came by it naturally. At my very first office job in an accounting office there was a clean desk policy. That meant when you left for the day or for lunch, everything was put away in its proper place in drawers and cupboards. I think we were allowed to leave a stapler and adding machine sitting out – and our telephone – but the desk was to be otherwise bare.

This practice has followed me throughout my life and I believe in it. For one thing, it allows you to find completion to your day or task to put away what you are finished with. And now you truly have a clean slate, as they say, to begin the next.

One of the team members at the office works part days and hasn't quite mastered this skill. I will walk by her desk and see files opened, binders stacked and eye glasses sitting as if she is just resting her eyes – and then be told she has left for the day. It just doesn't leave a good impression.

Don't fall for the idea either that a clean work space means you have nothing to do and should be given more tasks. Your work will speak for itself and those around you might get the hint they should tidy up a bit.

Chapter 71
Will Your Wishes

Nobody wants to think about their own mortality or how their loved ones will carry on after their departure from this earth. This is the reason a great many people do not have a written document – or will – expressing their wishes.

When my mother was ill and living her last few days with us, she mentioned very casually that she wanted to be laid to rest in the small town cemetery near to her home and not in the city one where the rest of the family had chosen. It was a shock to all of us, but we were grateful for the knowledge when it came time to make the arrangements. She had never bothered to write this down or tell us her wishes previously.

Creating a 'Last Will and Testament' as they are called need not be complicated or expensive. There are lots of versions at the book store or online you can use and we did this for many years before getting a formal document written up by a lawyer. You can even write a letter or a few notes yourself. The trick is making sure you have someone witness in writing your signature and that it is something you actually wrote.

The two other very important documents everyone needs is a Power of Attorney and a Personal Directive.

The first one is absolutely necessary if you are injured or sick and unable to speak your wishes. Your partner of family may not be able to pay your bills or make financial decisions for you without it! The latter tells the story of how you wish to be cared for medically when you cannot do this yourself.

Make it easy on your family and plan ahead with a few simple pieces of paper.

Chapter 72
Little Labels

On a recent holiday overseas, one of our stops was in a small village in France. A tiny shop offered homemade biscuits and treats, all organized into perfect bins with beautiful labels of each one's contents. It was so well-organized and made it easy for you to buy something. And of course we did!

If you have made it this far through these pages, you have probably also figured out I am a little bit extreme on neatness and organization. One of my favourite tools is a label maker and I use it often.

When we move across town or across the country, I label each box with every item that goes in it so we can easily remember where something is at the other end. There's nothing worse after a long day of moving than to not be able to find something you really need – closed boxes all look alike!

My pantry is organized into bins and jars for flour, sugar, nuts, pasta and many other things and each one has a label. It saves time when you are cooking and helps you avoid the nasty mistake of picking the wrong look-alike ingredient. And when it's time to buy more of something, it's easy to find the right place to put it.

I use my label maker to mark keys that I do not use all the time, so I can find the right one without a game. If an appliance has complicated instructions that I tend to forget – or if someone else is going to be using it in my absence – I put a little label on it with the necessary instructions in brief. The whole idea is to save yourself some time and money.

Chapter 73
A Knack for Notes

For some reason, I get my best ideas first thing in the morning and often while I am in the shower. And it's a really interesting conversation starter at the office when I begin with, "I was thinking about you in the shower this morning." But after the giggles, they are usually great ideas that I or others can use.

The trouble with my aging mind is that I sometimes don't remember these earth-shattering ideas for a great many minutes and have to write them down. So I keep a stack of sticky notes and a pen in the bathroom for this very reason. I also keep a stack on my bedside table, as often I get good ideas in the middle of the night and do not want to wake my partner by tapping away at my phone to electronically write a note or email. Good old paper and pen do the trick every time. Some days the ideas come fast and furious and I need several little stickies.

Since it's almost always with me, I also use my smart phone for this task throughout the day. I often send myself a dozen emails when I am away from home or the office to remember things to do or with ideas I have. And the 'note' function on my phone has literally thousands of entries!

I have read that successful people write down 10 new ideas each day. It makes sense since ideas roaming around in our brains usually find an escape route to nowhere and once they are committed to paper have a much higher chance of being acted upon.

Chapter 74
Compact Cleaning

Many years ago when the girls were small, we tried having a housekeeper. It seemed like a great idea until we realized we spent the entire evening before they were scheduled to come straightening up the house so they could find the floors and countertops to clean!

I am not sure I have ever met a person who loves to do housework and I am certainly not one of them. My partner does most of the actual cleaning in our house and I have learned that it's much easier to tackle the 'straightening' part – my job – in small bits.

Pick a room at a time or even go smaller – a drawer or a closet at a time – and straighten out the contents. I'm a fan of removing everything, going through it and then replacing only what is still needed or wanted. This is a good time to give the drawer or closet a good vacuum or washing as well. Then you will have room for a whole bunch more stuff that might be lying around the house in need of a resting spot.

Chapter 75
Keepsake King

Up until a few years ago, I was the king of keepsakes. I had every notebook, assignment and project from pre-school all the way to my final year of university. There were many large bins and all perfectly organized. Along with this forest worth of paper, there were almost the same number of containers with childhood keepsakes and toys. Since we were planning to downsize our home, it was time for me to address this!

It might not be the same for everyone, but I found it very painful to purge these things. Each item or page brought back a memory of some forgotten time and it felt like a piece of me was going into the trash or recycle bin each time I tossed something. And it took many weekends to finish the task!

Along the way I learned a few tricks and got some help from my friend and favourite artwork framer, Karen. She is the absolute master of being able to preserve a few treasured keepsakes behind glass. This turns them into wonderful pieces or art you and your family can enjoy every day instead of being packed away. Since I only saved a few things from the mountain of my past, I also saved my daughters from this awful task at some distant date!

I recommend you do the same for your own children. There is never any shortage of cute outfits, treasured toys and books and refrigerator-worthy artwork to keep from their younger days. These too can be made into a perfect piece of art they can enjoy forever.

Chapter 76
Fantastic Finances

When I was growing up, my mom was the keeper of the financial records in our home. Although she did not work outside our home after my sisters and I were born, she kept the family earnings on track and I always felt we lived very well despite being a one-income family. One of my clearest memories is seeing her hand over to my father a few bills as his 'allowance' after all the bills were paid. She didn't mess around!

Mom had a giant ledger with green paper like an old-school accountant would use and she entered every expense in detail. When I was old enough to have my first part-time job, I mirrored this practice with my own little ledger book. I have done this my whole life and now use a spreadsheet on my computer, but the process is the same.

By keeping track of your income and expenses, you start to see patterns that you are either pleased with or not. If you are spending too much in one area you can clearly see it and make alterations. Good records also ensure you never miss a bill payment, which can be the quickest way to a bad credit rating and a lifetime of paying more than you should when it comes time to borrow for a car or home.

One of the other uses of financial record keeping is to set goals. I saved for my first house my dividing each pay into actual envelopes for rent, groceries, clothing, entertainment and house savings. I never borrowed from the house envelope and was able to save enough in one year for the down payment.

In the last few years, I was delighted to see my oldest daughter had a sheet of paper tracking her part-time income and all her goals. The result for her was a summer of travelling overseas without ever incurring any debt. It made me a proud papa!

Chapter 77
No Isn't Negative

Many years ago when the girls were little, my former partner's family had a tradition on Christmas Eve where one of the uncles would dress up as Santa Claus and hand out little gifts to everyone. It seems like an innocent enough activity, but we hated it. There were many members of that family with which we did share common values and we really wanted to be at home with our young family creating our own traditions. It took a few years, but finally we said we would not be coming anymore.

It's difficult to say, "No." Our society promotes the idea that more is always better. Take just one more fitness class before the piano recital and after volunteering at the community centre. Three invitations for coffee on Sunday afternoon? No problem, you can fit them all in. Put the kids in hockey – and skiing – and skating – and basketball – and soccer – because you never know what they are going to be good at or enjoy so it's better to cover all the bases.

Mustering the courage to decline invitations and new commitments makes our lives 'simpler' and allows us to focus on what is really important. It gives us more time to read, sleep, learn, cook, have fun, be silent and love. Being away from all that busy-ness might just allow you to realize what you are really good at and where you want to take your life's goals next.

Be Culinary

Chapter 78
Butter Made Better

I am not sure why it took me until I was in my 40s to learn this one, but watching Chef Michael Smith on television one day gave me this revelation. If you are frying up some onions or chicken or almost anything else in butter, add a little olive oil to keep the butter from burning. The mixture of the two gives great flavour and no burnt mess. Nice!

Chapter 79
Garbage In, Garbage Out

Garbage in, garbage out (GIGO) was a term used a lot when I was a kid and first learning about computers. It meant that if you put data in that was garbage, the computer was going to give you back garbage. It was not a miracle worker.

Let's be clear – learning about computers way back then involved studying about machines that filled entire rooms. Our "computer" classes consisted of spending hours punching special cards that told the computer to do a complicated task such as adding 5 plus 7.

What I am referring to here, however, is the folly of making a recipe which contains an ingredient you don't like and believing that you will like the end result. It just doesn't work that way. Find a new recipe or substitute something you like and I promise you the result will be more appealing.

This goes the same way for ingredients you cannot pronounce or have never heard of. I have fallen into the trap of shopping all over town for these "special" ingredients for a recipe, only to hate the result and then finding the bottle, can or package languishing in my pantry or fridge several years later. Keep it simple and keep it to what you know you like!

Chapter 80
Rice Is Nice

My former partner studied at university to become a home economics teacher. It was surprising how little actual cooking they did in school, but she did come away with a few tricks I have never seen elsewhere. One of them was to cook your rice in the oven. No boiling, warnings against peeking or expensive rice cookers. It's brilliant.

Put your desired amount of rice into an oven-safe casserole dish and add twice as much water as the amount of rice. Put a lid on it. Bake it for one hour at 350 degrees and it is perfect every time. I have tried this with many different types of rice – white, brown, basmati, Asian – and it works brilliantly the same with each one.

Chapter 81
Roast Rules

We have an entire bookshelf in our home lined with cookbooks. Cooking is one of our favourite hobbies and allows us to eat much healthier than buying packaged meals. The oldest cookbook I own is one that I refer to very often and is aptly entitled Easy Basics.

A standby special meal for us is roast beef. I shied away from it for most of my life because of the way my mother – bless her heart – cooked the death out of it! But now I have the easiest and most never-fail way to prepare roast beef and everyone raves about it. Everyone should have a go-to entrée in their repertoire for when a new love, the in-laws or your boss are coming for dinner.

First of all, you need a good cut of beef and we always choose a standing rib or prime rib. It is, of course, one of the most expensive. But we only buy it when it is on sale or a good price at the butcher or grocery store.

Beef should always be at room temperature before you start to cook it, so take it out of the refrigerator at least 30 minutes before it is going into the oven. Then comes the seasoning and the rule is simple is always best. A little coarse salt, freshly cracked pepper and a good steak rub – the latter not also having salt as an ingredient.

Rub it all over the roast and let it sit a further 15 minutes or so at room temperature.

The roast is cooked in a shallow pan on a rack with nothing covering it – this part is essential, so invest in this type of pan if you do not already have one. The roast sits on the rack with the ribs down and the fat cap on top. This way the fat naturally bastes the meat as it cooks. Sometimes I get a roast that is a little lopsided and it wants to fall over! This can be solved by sitting an oven safe dish or measuring cup up against the roast for it to lean on. It's important, as you want the roast to stay 'fat up' while it cooks.

Cook the roast at 325 degrees for 25 minutes per pound (454 grams equals one pound). When the oven time is done, take the roast out and remove it from the pan to a cutting board, leaving it on the rack, and cover it with aluminum foil for about 10 minutes. This 'resting period" allows the juices to settle and not run all over the place when you carve it.

The resting period gives you time to make gravy out of the wonderful pan juices, if you desire. Another reason we love this recipe, especially for dinner parties, is most of the work is done in advance and you can socialize while the roast is in the oven. Potatoes and vegetables can be roasted at the same temperature too – for the last hour – and everything is ready at the same time!

After carving, keep the beef bones for soup or broth and you have the start of a whole other meal at a future date. They freeze well and for a long time.

Chapter 82
Scratch Success

A trip to the market or grocery store these days is an adventure into the world of convenience. Busy people demand fast and efficient products and manufacturers are right there to accommodate. But the downside is the preservatives and unknown ingredients in these products that give them everything from great colours to a long shelf life. Do you really want this stuff in your body?

You don't need to be a television network food star to have a few tricks up your sleeve and make some kitchen basics from scratch. Your body will thank you for the effort and your friends and family will rave at the results.

Let's start with a grocery store lesson. Most stores are laid out with the produce, fresh meats and bread around the perimeter of the building. That is where you should be shopping, avoiding the aisles in the middle as much as possible where all the packaged foods lay waiting with their strange ingredients.

But even in the produce aisle, they have snuck in all kinds of convenience foods. Avoid the packaged salads, perfectly shaped carrots and pre-cut veggies – they all contain things to keep them looking pretty way too long. Instead, buy fresh lettuces and vegetables and take a few minutes at home with a knife and cutting board!

If you like a nice salad dressing or dip, that too can easily be made at home and not be purchased in a bottle with an expiry date of five years hence. Combine three tablespoons of cider or wine vinegar with a teaspoon or more of mustard and then drizzle a half cup of olive oil into it while stirring to make a fantastic concoction. Add salt, pepper, garlic and whatever other spices you like to finish it off.

My favourite meal ever is good-old spaghetti and meat sauce and it's so easy to make yourself. Look for canned tomato sauce – preferably organic – that has no sugar and low sodium. Brown some ground beef or chicken with some chopped onions, celery and peppers and add the sauce. No need for a jar with the face of some fictitious Italian mother or famous chef on it!

Chapter 83
Tasty Treats

As a young boy, my maternal grandmother – Granny – lived just two houses down from us on the same street. Saturday was her shopping day and she almost always took me along. Our little secret was I could put almost anything I wanted in the shopping cart and she would keep it at her house for when I came over. The snack, candy and soda pop aisles at the grocery store were my weakness for many years!

I firmly believe that even junk food was less junky back then. The ingredient list on most so-called treats now is pretty scary. I've learned a few tricks to make simpler treats at home. While they are certainly not health food, at least I know what went in them. And simple to prepare is the name of the game.

Who can resist the smell of freshly popped popcorn? It's my favourite treat and I refuse to buy the pre-packaged microwave variety, although that is exactly where I make it. All you need is popcorn and a paper lunch bag. Put about one-third of a cup of popcorn in the bag and close the top with some kind of clip that is not metallic. About 3 minutes on the highest power does the trick – you'll want to listen for the popping to stop – and you have hot popcorn without any crazy additives. You can always add your own melted butter, salt or seasoning afterwards.

Another super easy treat to make is something I call ting-a-lings, but I have no idea where that name came from. They are made with equal amounts of four ingredients and you don't even really cook them! Melt semi-sweet chocolate and butterscotch chips in the microwave and then stir in chow mein noodles and salted peanuts. Put spoonfuls on a cookie sheet and put them in the refrigerator for a couple of hours. A half-cup of each ingredient makes about eight clusters.

Chapter 84
Pinch Your Portions

I really like sugar. I used to like it so much I could drink a can of cola in about 10 seconds. And drank it many times a day. I didn't understand that a bag of candy might be made for sharing and I could also eat the whole bag by myself in a few minutes.

But when my pant size started to grow and an uncomfortable middle section developed on my body, I started to learn about portion size. A little is okay and a lot is not.

The evils of sugar are becoming well-documented these days, but my point is not to judge what you decide to put in your mouth. One sip of a soda or a couple of candies from the bag will give you the same satisfaction on your tongue (and in your brain) as the whole thing. And last a lot longer in your desk, refrigerator or pantry!

Beyond the wonders of treats and desserts, watching one's portion size of all food is extremely beneficial in weight management and one of the hardest things to do.

As a child, my mom would fill our plates for us with the amount of food she thought we should eat and for the size of the plate or bowl. And doing the best they could with their Great Depression-raised knowledge, my parents did not allow us to leave the table until we had finished everything on our plates. My sister still tells the story of sitting at the dinner table at midnight in the dark because she had not finished her peas!

They say old habits are hard to break and this one still haunts me to this day. It doesn't matter if you served yourself or the chef at your favourite restaurant filled the plate, finishing what is in front of you when you are no longer hungry is bad. One tip is to use a smaller plate or bowl to begin with. Another is to drink a big glass of water before you start eating.

Chapter 85
Recipe Repeat

My sister-in-law gave my partner one of the most wonderful gifts for Christmas a few years ago – a binder full of all their mother's hand-written recipes. It's both a treasured keepsake and well-used reference piece in our home. There is nothing better than a tried and true recipe with food stains on it!

Sharing recipes is almost a religion with our family and friends – if it tastes good and turns out successfully it is fair game for someone else to try as well. So unless you are *Coca-Cola or Colonel Sanders*, don't be afraid to share a recipe and ask for one in return. When I write or type a recipe, I always name it with the giver's name so I can remember its origins.

Be Domestic

Chapter 86
Learn to Launder

My friend Kelly is one of the most organized people I know and packs 36 hours of work and life into every 24-hour day. But I was really surprised at what I found in her washing machine one time when we were visiting her home on the West coast. She told us to go ahead and put anything we wanted into the washing machine and just take out whatever previous load was in there and put it in the dryer.

Everything was in there. Towels, bed sheets, dark clothing, white clothing and maybe even a pair of sneakers. It was so packed full that I don't know how there was any room left for water or movement. It was like unpacking Mary Poppins bag when we pulled the menagerie all out.

So here's the rule. Always sort your colours & darks from your whites. This keeps your whites looking white and white lint off your darks. Don't overload the washing machine. It does its job by sloshing the water and soap through the fibers of your clothes and it can't do that if everything is a big glob of fabric-ness.

Use a small amount of soap and never the giant scoop the soap manufacturer provides in the box or recommends on the bottle. Unless you are digging ditches, your clothes are not that dirty. Excess soap will not rinse out and will stay on your clothes and in the machine and pipes and make them yucky. That's the technical term.

There is not much that really needs to be washed in hot water, but doing so for your towels will make them come out fresh and not musty smelling. I don't know the technical reason. My mom taught me this and it just works.

Chapter 87
Renting Relieves

There is likely no bigger dream for most North Americans than owning their own home. I am guessing it comes from a combination of our pioneering ancestors who arrived only a few hundred years ago and the vast amount of open land available. I do know my friends overseas do not always aspire to this same goal.

As a young man, it was made very clear to me that the programmed course of life was to only rent a home for a short period of time until one had saved enough for a down payment on the purchase of a home. I remember well my parents had one set of friends that rented their homes. It stood out in my memory because it was so unconventional, since everyone else in their circle of friends owned their homes.

But there is another way of thinking and its worth putting out there as an alternative. Many people will never actually 'own' their home because the mortgage payments are too large and will last well beyond their income-earning years. So are they not just renting from the bank?

I once read an article where the author compared home ownership to a refrigerator. His point was you need a refrigerator to keep your food fresh and when it stops working or is too small you get a new one. Your home should be like a refrigerator for you and your belongings and nothing more. It will wear out and need replacing and it's easier to move on to a new one and let the home owner deal with the repairs needed.

I merely offer this point of view as food for thought. Home ownership can be very rewarding and I have done it for most of my life while raising a family. But in today's changing world of multiple careers and ease of travel perhaps stopping off in a variety of locations – and renting a property while there – has some merit.

Chapter 88
Golden Guidance

Have you ever pulled an item from the refrigerator or pantry to find the lid loose and it spills on you or falls? Or visited the washroom to find a bare cardboard roll on the tissue holder and no sign of a replacement? My guess is this is fairly frustrating to you and others.

The Golden Rule, originally attributed to Jesus himself, says something like you should treat others like you wish to be treated yourself. It's a bit like the 'walking in someone else's shoes' scenario and requires that you give some thought to how you are leaving a situation for the next person who encounters it.

Try to go through life as if you are not the only participant! Tighten that jar lid and replace that bathroom tissue roll. Put the toilet seat down when you are finished. Re-hang the towel the same way you found it. Empty the dishwasher when it's clean and turn it on when you fill it with the last dish that will possibly fit. Re-fill the ice cube tray when you take the last few cubes. Make more coffee at the office when you take the last cup.

I could go on for pages, but you get the idea. Be a good prophet and set an example for others as the one who always leaves a situation as good or better than you found it.

Chapter 89
Live By Lists

We have a great 'big box' retailer in our town and visit it frequently. But it can be a dangerous place without a plan and a list. Of course, the retailer knows this very well and counts on emotional and spontaneous purchases. That's why they rearrange the store every week and put the newest and niftiest items right out front where you will see them!

I never cross the threshold of this place without a list of what I need. Of course there is a little browsing, but I try my best to stick to the list – and my budget – to avoid walking out the door with 12 chickens, a case of motor oil and a new 50-inch television.

Lists help not only make your shopping visit more efficient, they assist you in not wasting money on things that will perish before you can use them. Another list I make is a meal plan for the week, so I know what we are making for breakfast, lunch and dinner and the needed supplies before I head to the store.

My former in-laws had a freezer that was the size of a small car and I never really understood why two people needed that much frozen food. My experience has revealed that most fresh meat and many vegetables do not necessarily benefit from freezing. My list helps me buy just enough fresh food for the week so preserving it for another life is not required.

Chapter 90
Love Local

When I was renovating our first home many years ago, we ate out in restaurants a great deal. I would work at my office job all day and then come home and put on some old blue jeans and a t-shirt and get to work. Time was of the utmost importance because otherwise we would be living in a half-renovated house forever!

More often than not, we would go to our neighbourhood pizza place for a quick bite after the evening's work was done. They soon knew us by name, along with our favourite dishes, and we knew them just as well. There was a certain comfort in not making a dining decision later at night and never being concerned about what kind of food or service we would receive.

As time went on, this same restaurant was our go-to with our young daughters. They knew my oldest girl would not eat anything on the menu and brought her chopped fresh tomatoes. That was what she liked and gobbled them up.

The renovations also meant I needed the assistance and advice of good hardware stores, and found a plumbing shop nearby that I seemed to visit almost daily. Once again, they knew me well, assisted me greatly and even loaned me tools from time to time. In return, they got all my plumbing business.

The world is a big place and getting smaller every day with all the great technology we have. But nothing beats patronizing your local merchants and getting to know them. The service you will receive from someone who knows you will always be better and you might even get a lower price every now and then. And even if the price doesn't beat the competition, it feels great to support a local business person who lives right in your community.

Chapter 91
Location Lasts

When my life was in transition a few years ago, I purchased a condominium for myself in a newly-built high-rise building. It had all the bells and whistles, including a gorgeous view of the mountains to the west. What I hadn't noticed or considered when I made the choice was the extreme heat the west-facing orientation would bring to my home or the earth-rattling noise of the railroad tracks running one block away from the building.

Most of us have heard the three rules of buying real estate – location, location and location. And whether you are buying a piece of property in which to live, renting a home or setting up a business this rule never fails. Choose wisely when it comes to what you are near to, the way the sun rises and sets and any busy streets or industry close by that might affect your enjoyment.

The other sometimes overlooked piece of the location equation is to whom you are going to live near. I am not trying to be a snob with this advice! But if you do not want to live near less-desirable people then you can't purchase the bargain home in the less-desirable area. You alone will not bring up the average in the neighbourhood. Consider your values and how you want you and your family to live and choose accordingly, even if it stretches your budget for the short term.

Chapter 92
Grow a Garden

We have always lived in an area that is not particularly conducive to growing things outdoors, with only about 50 frost-free days per year. But one of my fondest memories is my mom heading to the garden centres in mid-May each year to pick out an array of bedding out plants. They were put out for a few hours each day to 'harden off' and then tucked away in the garage again at night because it was still too cold to plant.

Despite the less-than-perfect conditions, Mom's garden always looked spectacular all summer and along the way I inherited a very small part of the gardening gene. In the third grade, we all came home with an evergreen tree one day and quickly planted it in our yard. The three trees of slightly different sizes, representing my sisters and me, still stand in the yard at the old family home.

I love having a few plants to nurture through the season and, more recently, even tried my hand at growing a few vegetables and herbs that helped with the grocery bill. The herbs were plentiful enough to be harvested and dried to use over the winter.

So wherever you live and no matter how small your abode, have a garden. It can be as small as a couple of pots on your window ledge or balcony – or as large as a full-fledged effort that can feed the family. There is something very rewarding and in our DNA about planting a tiny seed or seedling and watching it grow into something bigger with a bit of sun, water and love. Even the things that don't grow teach us something. It's a metaphor of life itself.

Be Fashionable

Chapter 93
Choose Colour

If you have to make a choice between a selection of colours where black, brown or grey are included, always choose colour.

If the colour decision is for the interior walls of your home, however, stick with basic whites, taupes and off-whites and accent with colour in your furniture or accessories.

Chapter 94
Odd Is In

When you are placing decorative items on a shelf, table or mantel, arrange them in groups of threes or other odd numbers. It makes them more visually appealing and memorable. The items don't have to be the same or even the same size – in fact, it looks better if they are all different sizes and heights.

Chapter 95
Dress for Success

My parents were not wealthy by any means, but I do remember them always looking like a million bucks. My childhood years were still the days when people dressed up to go shopping, to church or to a concert. And one would never consider getting on an airplane in anything less than formal dress!

Our little home had one bathroom for my parents and three kids, but I can still see my mother perfecting her make-up in a tiny mirror and choosing a dress like it was the most important decision of the decade.

I have learned a few basic things along the way, and, of course these are going to be mostly for the male readers. You ladies have a billion magazines to read for this kind of stuff and a bunch of girlfriends to correct you if you get it wrong!

So gentlemen, here we go. Your belt colour should always match your shoe colour. And those shoes should always be polished. I know the days of polishing our shoes on Sunday nights are long gone, but keep some of those pop-up leather wipes at the ready. Or like my former boss did, keep an old sock with some clear polish in a bottom drawer. I read somewhere once that your shoes are the first thing people look at after your face. Hmm.

On a long sleeved shirt, the placket buttons (those little ones on your sleeve) should always be done up. In fact, all those extra buttons on a dress shirt should be fastened. And of course your shirt is always neatly pressed.

The rule for your suit jacket or blazer front buttons is also very easy. There are usually three buttons and, counting from the top, they should be fastened always, sometimes and never. If there are only two or perhaps four buttons, you can still follow the same rule.

Chapter 96
Sole Searching

There are a few times in life where the advice you may have been given by your parents is incorrect. Buying new shoes is one of those times. The days are also mostly gone where a sales person helps you choose your shoes and makes sure you have the correct size. So it's all up to you.

Here's my two cents. Shoes that aren't comfortable in the store will not get more comfortable after you buy them. All of that, "They will soften up," or "You will grow into them," advice was bunk. I'm sorry. I have too many pairs of worn-once shoes and too many foot scars to believe this.

When you can, always buy leather shoes or at least those with leather uppers. Man-made materials will cause your feet to sweat and be stinky! And despite being cheaper to purchase, they will not last near as long as the leather counterpart.

Chapter 97
Tear Out the Tags

I have only every worn men's clothes, so I am not certain if it is the goal of clothing manufacturers to punish all of humanity or just men. In particular, I have an issue with tags in men's garments.

Sometimes there are tags on the inside of collars that scratch and rub one's neck raw. Sometimes there are tags on inside shirt seams that tickle and scratch your ribs. One least favourite is tags placed too close to the top of trouser waist bands so that it looks like your underwear is showing. And how about tags with extra buttons attached that make unsightly and uncomfortable lumps? I could go on.

My advice is to put the piece of clothing on at home after the purchase and at a time when you are not rushing to get ready for work, school or a date. Take a moment to feel all those annoying tags against your body and then remove the item from your body and cut them all out! If you need to save some of them to remember care instructions or to preserve those extra buttons for when you will need them, attach the removed tag to an index card with tape or a staple and identify the clothing item. It's better in a drawer than bothering you all day.

Chapter 98
Give to Get

A few years ago we came home from a vacation to find our clothes closet rod had pulled off the wall and collapsed on the floor, taking everything with it. That was a pretty clear sign we had too many clothes in that closet and it was time to purge!

All of us have clothing we don't wear very often or at all, but keep it for when we lose weight, when we gain weight or when we get invited to that special event. A trick I learned to actually keep track of the things we never wear is to turn all the hangers backwards. This was easy for us on this particular occasion since everything was lying on the floor!

As you wear things and re-hang them, you obviously hang them back up the right way. At end of one year – or whatever amount of time you decide – you will clearly see all the items you have not worn by the still-backwards hangers.

If you have great pieces of clothing that are still in good shape and in style, find yourself a good tailor to make alterations. You might be surprised how little it costs to have something taken in or out and then you have a brand new item to add to your wardrobe.

You will still need to use some of your own willpower to say goodbye to clothing and I struggle with this. But if you find a good organization that takes used clothing, it makes the giving away that much easier. In our community we have a Dream Centre that provides education and residence to re-integrate disadvantaged people back into the community. They are always incredibly grateful for the clothes we bring to them and our items get a second chance as well.

Chapter 99
Fantastic Furniture

When I was growing up, my mom would re-arrange the furniture in the living room of our 800 square-foot house several times a year. You could always tell it was "that time" when you came home from school to find things in new spots or, if she was not quite finished, in a pile in the middle of the floor. How she did this so creatively in such a small space is a mystery to me now that I have had several of my own homes of various sizes.

Mom was not alone in this endeavor either. My bedroom window looked across to the kitchen window of our neighbour Phyllis. I could always tell when she was rearranging if I saw a large lamp or vase suddenly sitting on the kitchen table awaiting a new home.

An empty room can be either an opportunity or challenge, depending on how you approach it. This can be fun stuff if you let your creativity go crazy and follow a few basic rules.

Start with how the room will be used and how many people will use it. This will tell you what type and how much seating is required. Think about how you will add more seating for larger gatherings, either with pull-out or hidden seating (large cushions that can become floor seating?) or with chairs you can bring in.

Next is identifying the room's focal point. Is it a fireplace, window, television or a music system? If it has multiple focal points, you are going to have to choose the most important and orient the furniture toward that one. This is where I could go on my rant about how tacky and awful it is to hang a TV over a fireplace to give two focal points equal priority. But I will resist. Or did I?

You will want to place the largest pieces of furniture into the room first – like a sofa in the living room or a bed in the bedroom. Try to stay away from pushing all the furniture against the walls! If you have the flexibility, two love seats placed across from each other or a large sofa with smaller chairs creates a nice balance. I love the idea and look of a bed angled in a room with the headboard away from the wall, but have never had a room big enough in which to try it.

Try to place a table or some horizontal surface next to every seat so people have a place to set a beverage, book, eye glasses, cell phone or other electronic device. Keep in mind the scale of your pieces too. Don't put all the tall stuff on one side and short stuff on the other. Instead balance the room with tall across from tall and short across from short, if possible. This allows the eyes to move around the room and enjoy all of it.

I can almost guarantee my Mom never did this, but give your body a break. Measure the room's dimensions as well as those of your furniture pieces and then draw a quick sketch of the space or use computer software. Graph paper, a pencil and a big eraser are great old-fashioned tools for this. Remember to show electrical outlets, windows and other features or obstructions. It's easier to move things around on paper first!

Finally, remember that like in nature, the greatest spaces evolve over time. Let your home décor come together slowly. Don't feel you have to fill every wall and every space right away. It's much better if some of the pieces reflect your personality, your experiences and your journey through life.

Chapter 100
Art at the Eye

If you want your home to look like an interior designer helped you out, hang artwork so the top of the artwork (not the frame or the mat) is at eye level. If you are very short or very tall, error on the side of a person who is about 5 feet, 9 inches tall. If you have a set of smaller art that you are hanging in a vertical row together, the centre piece should be at eye level with the other pieces above and below.

When hanging art or a mirror over a fireplace mantle the top of the piece will usually be much higher than eye level. Hang your art so there is about seven inches between the bottom of the piece and the mantle and it will look perfect.

Chapter 101
Get Good at Gratitude

Do you only give thanks when there is a turkey and stuffing in front of you? It took me a long time to learn to be grateful for every day and everything in it. There are many quotes and thousands of books written on this "glass half-full" mentality, but I found the best thing little tool is to keep a gratitude journal.

Start with the big lumpy bits and work your way down. Are you grateful for your spouse or partner? For your kids? How about your job or profession? If you are only grateful for certain parts of these things, separate those out.

Read your list often and make changes to it as great things get added to your life. If a relationship or job ends, write down your gratitude for the opportunity to start a new one. It's a wonderful feeling to remind yourself of the things for which you are thankful.

Chapter 102
Don't Wait to Live

Sometimes it seems I have been waiting my whole life to live. I am a professional at counting the days, weeks and months until some milestone has passed and I can finally live.

When I graduate from high school. When that bully moves away. After graduation from university. As soon as I get my first full-time job. After I get married. When I buy my first house. As soon as this car loan is paid off. When the kids are old enough to be left alone. When my sister Patti recovers from brain cancer. When I recover from her death. After my mom gets better from her breast and lung cancer. As soon as I move on from watching her die. When I find the courage to leave this bad marriage. As soon as I meet someone new. After we find a new place to live. When the mortgage is paid off. After I retire.

Do you have a list like this? Almost all of us do, but the secret to a happy life is to live each day and stop worrying about the past or the future. Actor Robin Williams' famous "Carpe diem – seize the day" speech from the movie *Dead Poets Society* is something we should all watch again and again. He reminds the boys in his class that if they wait too long to accomplish great things, they will be nothing but fertilizer for daffodils.

The anxiety we feel ends when we stop worrying about the future or waiting for some perfect future after all the "stuff" is over. The stuff is life! Live each day – the present is all that matters. Like the Tim McGraw country song says, "Live like you were dying." Dale Carnegie wrote in his 1948 book How to Stop Worrying and Start Living, "Live in day-tight compartments. Don't stew about the future. Just live each day until bedtime."

Chapter 103
Whistling Works

Walt Disney's *Snow White* made famous the song *Whistle While You Work* in the 1937 animated classic as she made it fun to clean up the seven dwarfs' cottage. Miss White was trying to impart that any mundane task can be made better while humming a little tune or whistling a few bars.

As a young boy I could not whistle. It drove me crazy and I would practice in front of a mirror for hours. Eventually I learned to whistle by sucking in instead of blowing out – yes weird, I know! And soon I was whistling like a pro.

I am still a whistler and often do it without even realizing it. People will often comment, "You're so happy all the time with your whistling." What they might not realize is that whistling or humming or singing can MAKE you happy. It sends a message to your brain that is good, despite the fact that whatever situation or job you are doing may not be.

Who knew Snow White was such a happiness guru?

Chapter 104
Dating Never Dies

Who among us doesn't remember their first date? Deciding where to go. The grooming. The dressing and re-dressing. The worrying about whether or not they would like you or you like them. Some of us did a lot of it and some not very much.

If you are lucky enough to have a great partner as I do – or when you do – my recommendation is to never stop dating. Show up with flowers when they least expect it. Go out to a movie or concert or dinner often. Stay in and cook something decadent that you seldom have. Have a junk food night. Go for a long drive.

Being in a committed relationship doesn't mean that all the fun has stopped. Date nights bring back those butterflies in the stomach along with new conversations and will help the two of you fall in love all over again.

Chapter 105
Silly Songs

As a young father I treasured the times alone with my daughters when we could be silly together. At first it was just me being silly with a baby that could only coo and giggle in response. It helped me relax in a role that was very new to me and stop taking myself so seriously.

My daughters still remember the silly diaper-change song I made up and sang each time the task was required. For years we joked that I would sing it at their weddings, but so far I have refrained. I would sing my own versions of the ABC song as we walked around the neighbourhood, marching to the beat and hoping the alphabet would sink into their little minds.

As they grew, we added silly song time in the bathtub – all of us wearing our swimsuits and splashing around to our favourite songs from the radio, the words to which we had carefully memorized.

So be silly with your children – and yourself – and make up some YouTube-worthy song creations in the process!

Chapter 106
Best Backwards

I was a bit too young to be a full-blown Beatles fan, but I remember in the mid-1960s my sisters giggling about how you could play one of their albums backwards and hear messages. It was called 'backmasking' and some artists did actually record sounds or words backwards on a track of music.

I have found that doing things backwards in life is sometimes a great way to give you a fresh perspective. Recently on my lunchtime walk, for example, I had an errand to run at the beginning and ended up walking my usual route in the opposite direction. Although I have walked this way hundreds of times, I was surprised at the new things I saw and the views from the other direction! If there is something you do routinely, try doing it backwards and you might see something new as well.

Another trick I have used when I am bored with the way a room looks, or can't quite get the décor looking the way I like, is to look at it through a mirror. It sounds a bit weird, but it works. Carry a small handheld mirror around the room and look at everything backwards and you will be surprised at what you see.

Chapter 107
Traditions Treat

I would be the first to admit I am a person who loves routines and is just a little bit obsessive about them. But traditions are different from rituals and something I believe have a place in every family. Besides bringing happiness and comfort each time they occur, traditions are a base to which you can return in times of trouble or loss.

When my daughters were very young, we always said the same thing to them at bedtime as we departed after all the story time and tucking and multiple cups of water. "Night night. I love you. See you in the morning." Soon they would say the same thing back and we still to this day share the same salutation when we leave each other after an evening together.

The holidays have their own traditions for many families and ours is no exception. On Christmas Eve we give each other a tree ornament that has some symbolic relevance to the year just past. When the girls left home for the first time, they had a couple of dozen tree ornaments for their own homes, all with special meaning.

We host a party for friends and family each year on almost the same date and everyone looks forward to the event and to the homemade fudge they take home at the end of the night. Christmas morning for us means homemade cinnamon buns and New Year's Eve means watching *The Sound of Music* for the umpteenth time. Pick your own or borrow from your extended family or friends. The best ones get passed from generation to generation.

Chapter 108
Associate Attentively

Most of us have heard the advice to choose our friends wisely. But sometimes it doesn't feel like a choice we are consciously making. We work or go to school with people all day and assume they are our friends. We attend church or activities with people and assume because we have like interests that we will be friends. Usually time is the best judge of whether someone is an acquaintance or a real friend.

I am no philosopher, but the law of association basically states that you will become who you hang out with! Smokers attract smokers. Gamblers attract gamblers. Bullies attract bullies. Negative attracts negative. It works the same for the good stuff.

As a youth I was surprised how this theory played out mostly without me even realizing it. None of my friends smoked cigarettes and neither did I. None of my friends used drugs and neither did I. On a lighter note, none of my friends were snow skiers and neither was I. Most of my friends were at the top of their class academically. We liked going to movies and concerts and having dinner in nice restaurants. Hmm – nothing has changed for me!

Basically be around people who are kind to you and love you. You should feel better after every encounter with a true friend and not worse. People who are not kind to you will make you unkind, unhappy and unsuccessful.

Chapter 109
Complaining Is Draining

It's funny how travelling on an airplane can give you such a great chance to study human nature. I guess it's because there is a large group of people crammed into a small space for a relatively long time.

On a recent flight I witnessed several people complaining about the delay in our departure time. Some others whined about the lack of seat-back televisions and no internet connectivity. Others griped about the food and beverage choices on this particular flight.

As I assessed the situation, I wanted to say to them, "You do realize, don't you, that we are flying through the air in a metal tube and that alone is nearly a miracle?" But I did not say this to them.

My point is complaining does not solve anything except perhaps to incite those around you to join in. None of the crew on the airplane or even the staff back in the airline's office could possibly do anything to change these situations. Complaining is draining. Blaming is draining. Explaining is draining.

Chapter 110
Space for Solace

When my daughters were young, one of their favourite animated shows was called Little Bear. Little Bear lived in the forest and had many animal friends – and one little girl – with which he shared all his adventures. My personal favourite character was Frog, who dispensed Zen-like wisdom between his meditations. He lived at Little Bear's favourite swimming spot, Hop-Frog Pond, and often encouraged everyone to "be one with the log."

We all need to find time and a place to be one with our logs. One of my not-so-secret indulgences is to have a warm bath at the end of the day. It is made better if a wonderful-smelling candle is burning and some soft music is playing. It's my time alone and my thoughts can wander. Often I fall asleep. I have not yet drowned.

Another is to take a walk outside on my lunch break. I am very fortunate to work close to a riverbank pathway I can enjoy for over 30 minutes without encountering any traffic. And I think I have already mentioned how much I love to roll over and sleep late!

Find out what works for you, your schedule and your family. Making the time to be alone with your thoughts pays off in so many ways.

Chapter 111
Live Laugh Love

One of the saddest days of my life was the day I said goodbye to my mom. A few days later, in the middle of a March snowstorm, the minister spoke to a packed chapel of her family and friends. He spoke of nothing but love. I will never forget it.

Love is really all there is. There have been millions of songs, poems and books written about it throughout the ages. Love fuels us to get up, dress up and show up. It's the reason we come home at the end of the day. It's the basis of all religions. It's why I wrote these words in this book.

Choose love over all else, especially hate. Laugh along the way. Have an amazing life.

The End